MW01236077

We all desire to have longevity. Longevity in anything is desperately needed, and it is rare in today's leadership landscape! Tone Setters help us gain the insights and truths necessary for longevity in any stage and area of life. I have had the honor and privilege to know and serve with Jason Smith as his Executive Pastor for five years and never, while doing life as closely as people do in high levels of leadership, have I ever witnessed Jason compromise his character, his integrity, or his passion for seeing people come to know King Jesus and live a life of true freedom. Jason desires to help people realize that longevity often comes only from one's ability to show character through any situation. He brings to this book a lifetime and wealth of experience and openness that is profoundly needed in today's literature on leadership.

Tone Setters is a perfect blend of truth, grace, humor, and biblical perspective. Jason shows a vulnerability that few leaders do, and the outcome combines freshness and inspiration. Tone Setters is the perfect book for anyone seeking to develop, protect, or learn about healthy influence and character. I believe many pastors, leaders, and people of influence in any theater or season will benefit from the bits of truth that Jason unpacks and reminds us of in each chapter. I am better from reading this book. My marriage is healthier, and my influence is protected. Suppose you are up for a challenge, something different, and desire a book filled with a helpful perspective that will fuel longevity. In that case, you will need this book in your arsenal of yearly reads. Give it to your staff, team, or kids. I know I plan to!

Ted Leith

Executive Pastor

Latitude Church

TONE SETTERS

This book is dedicated to my precious wife, cheerleader, accountability partner, and best friend, Christina. Thank you for loving me unconditionally and for your support over these years. Your grace for me has covered many of my flaws and has helped me to grow and mature. I couldn't do nor want to do this life without you. I also dedicate this book to my sons, Garrison and Chandler. You have made me the most blessed and proud dad on the planet. You taught me much about being a husband, dad, pastor, and friend. Most importantly, you have taught me to love your mother like Jesus.

A huge thank you to the most talented, Jesus-loving staff I could ever lead. Thank you for supporting my dreams and for the vision you have had for this book. I pray that I am the leader I have written about and that you experience my support for you daily. I value and love you all dearly and am so thankful to get to do life with you.

To Latitude Church, thank you for allowing me to be your pastor. You all are my family. I love each of you and want God's very best for you. Thank you for laughing at my jokes and continuing to come back for more. God has truly blessed me with you, and I

can't wait to see what all God has next for us. Till the
nets are full!

Table of Contents

Introduction: Self-control helps keep you in control

Introduction:

This book is for pastors, elders, deacons, parents, and leaders inside and outside the church to protect their families, marriages, ministry, and most importantly, the kingdom of God they represent! The writing of this book was inspired after my heart had been ripped out from my chest, stomped on, dissected, and left to beat on its own through the many moral failings of pastors and leaders over me in past years. I want this book to be presented the way Jesus came to teach, with truth and grace. You can't have truth without grace, and grace can't work without truth. They go hand in hand. Praise God for both of them and the freedom we have through them. If you are reading this book, I hope that it challenges you. I also pray that this book protects you. I pray that it restores you. I pray this book will help heal someone's marriage, stop an ongoing affair, and repair what the enemy has attempted to devour. However, I mostly pray that you, my friend, will hear from God and be redeemed.

I was inspired to write this book because I am a pastor and desperately want to see and experience revival before Jesus comes back. I have prayed and fasted for revival for many years. I have seen glimpses of it, heard stories of small outbreaks, and our church has even witnessed a mighty move of God! But I crave revival! Do you know what revival really is? It's bringing life back to something that once was living. To revive means to give something life again. I am not talking about a crusade where an evangelist preaches the Gospel and thousands are saved. I believe in that, too. I am talking more about the church, the pastors and leaders, the ones who profess but struggle to possess. I am talking about the ones who preach weekly sermons telling people to get right, yet they are wrong. Those who teach lessons to the congregations but are not applying the lessons themselves. Parents who are parenting and still not following their parenting. For some reason, many pastors feel as if they are immune to attacks, immune to sin, immune to moral failures, and walk around with their/heads in the clouds.

I want to encourage all of us to walk in our calling again. I want all of us to have a fresh start, a new beginning, and a reason to wake up and stop complaining about burnout. I want all of us to be healthy and joyful and lead the people of God as Jesus did. Because you, my friend, are a tone setter!

Tone setter: A person or thing that determines or establishes a quality, feeling, or attitude to be followed subsequently. - Merriam Webster

Chapter 1

"It's time to set the tone."

We had what our church called a Team Night a couple of years ago. This was a designated night when the different serving teams of our church came together for a night of encouragement, refreshment, and an intentional time of team building. This particular Team Night was for our worship, production, and creative teams. I had prayed that the Holy Spirit would deposit a word inside of me to give that word to the teams.

As the night progressed, I had not yet received the "word." I kept praying as we kept encouraging and worshipping. Finally, the Holy Spirit gave me the word. He said: These people are the tone setters for the work I desire to do in and through them and our church. Tone setters, I silently repeated. My dad would always say to our baseball team before a game: "Set the tone!" Of course, as a kid that would rather play the sport than get taught dugout sayings of the sport, I didn't quite understand what my dad meant. His pregame speech for me as I took the mound to pitch sounded like this; "Let that first pitch set the tone. Let them know that we came to win. Get way ahead of the batter, so they get way behind in the count." However, this is what he was really saying: "You be the one that establishes the attitude and the direction this game should go and don't allow the other team to do that for you." Then, I understood! So, I would throw my best, fastest pitch first to let the opposing team know that we are here and intend to leave with a win in the books.

That Team Night, I told them they were tone setters. Their authority, their leadership, their attitude, their anointing, and surrender to Jesus would be what set the tone for others to follow and for how others would worship. Whatever tone is set for us will typically be what we will follow. Will it be an upbeat Holy Spirit-filled tone? Or, will it be a negative unpersuasive tone that would be followed? Whatever tone is set will be the tempo in which we will go. They were pretty fired up, knowing God would call them tone setters. They even took it a step further and printed it above the creative office door for all to see. It was pretty powerful!

Did you know that as a leader, missionary, front office secretary, worship leader, evangelist, and especially a pastor - you are a tone setter? In light of the past couple of years with the devastating, heartbreaking, and church-wrenching news of pastors having affairs, sleeping with members of their churches, and having the audacity to blame it only on depression, anxiety, or the devil, I felt in my spirit to put pen to paper. Now, I am by no means sinless or attempting to turn the spotlight on others' sins and flaws. I believe God is telling me several things that He wants us all to hear but, most importantly, to apply. Application is more profitable than information. Information lies dormant until there is a transformation. As a pastor myself, I have to understand the severity that comes along with my calling. I must realize that just because God has chosen me doesn't give me immunity from temptation or evil, nor does it take away my testosterone-driven desires. I am still a man! And I would add that I'm very thankful to be a man. I just have to keep reminding myself that I am nothing more than a servant of king Jesus, and to the people, He has entrusted me to shepherd. Wait, did I say servant? Yes, I did. I know not many pastors and leaders will read this book; actually, most likely, my wife will be the only one to read it, but I pray that every pastor and leader that does read this would hear my heart in what God has led me to write, take a self-evaluation and possibly repent. Actually, after reading this book, buy a copy for every elder, deacon, ministry leader, manager, supervisor, dentist, and chiropractor. If they are like me, they will understand its value.

First, I want to address the servanthood of the pastor. Before you read any further, stop and pray. Ask the Holy Spirit to remove any pride you may have right now. Ask Him to help you receive what is written throughout this book. Here we go! Are you ready?

Question: Do you remember where you were and what you did when God called you to pastor or lead? Now, I am assuming that God called you, and your great aunt Emma Jean wasn't the one who prophesied over you, and that was your confirmation. If God did call you into the pastorate, keep reading. If you know that He didn't call you, it's ok to get out now while the getting is good. I promise you can still go to heaven and still serve in the parking lot. That's a joke about serving in the parking lot. We could use you in the nursery! But seriously, if you are pastoring for any reason other than being a servant, please protect your family, the people at your church, and the kingdom of God and resign tonight. You will have peace, the church will flourish, and Jesus will bless you. All right, let's move on.

Even Jesus said that he didn't come to be served but to be a servant and to give his life as a ransom for many. The King of kings came to be a servant. He came to heal and bind up wounds. He came to feed, rescue, and wash people's feet. He came to dine with sinners. He came to be the light in the darkness. He came to see the needs and help meet their needs. He didn't send his disciples, XP, secretary, youth pastor, interns, or women's ministry to do the dirty work. He got filthy! He set up the tables. He pulled the weeds. He had conversations in the lobby and didn't hide in the green room like Bon Jovi on tour. He wasn't trying to be a superstar. He was the Bright Morning Star. He was willing to go, not just tell others what to do. He showed us what and how to do it. His life as a servant was our blueprint for becoming a servant. If you have gotten too big, too proud, or too afraid to serve the people in your church, find some feet to wash! If you can't carry on a conversation with the extra grace required for a patron of your church, find some feet to wash! If you aren't willing to pick up an empty cup, trash on the floor, or wipe urine off a toilet seat, find some feet to wash. I've never heard of a servant who never serves like The Servant - King Jesus. Don't call yourself a servant if you are unwilling to get dirty. I know what you're thinking: This is why I pay somebody to clean, so I don't have to. That is not the point of cleaning. The point is to have a servant's heart and a servant's attitude. I once served on a church staff for five years and never saw the senior pastor in a single church workday. I never saw him at a church-wide event. I often wondered what kind of servant he was until, after years, I never saw him serve alongside his team. Then I knew!

If you are one of those pastors that love to make your outreach numbers inflate by giving more tasks to others in your community or workplace, please don't post a selfie as if you've done something. Maybe I'm being a little harsh, but somebody has to say it. Maybe it sounds judgmental, but you all know what I'm talking about. Perhaps it's hitting a nerve right now. I pray that it is. Maybe you used to do those things, but now your pride, arrogance, and self-pity have turned your servanthood into a dictatorship. That is even worse! My greatest recommendation is to do as Jesus did; Go find some feet to wash. Weep before the Lord and your congregation. Get off of Instagram and wash some feet! (We will hit Instagram in the coming chapter. Don't go anywhere!!)

A shepherd serves. A shepherd or overseer or any kind of leader serves. You show me someone who serves, and I will show you a future leader. As a follower of Jesus, serving should be in our DNA. We shouldn't have to be begged, coerced, or paid to serve. We should be ready to serve God and his people. A pastor who doesn't serve can't only count preaching on Sundays as his service to the church. Oh, snap! Most likely, your paycheck is based on your job title and description, "pastor." In other words, It's not just preaching. If the truth is known, most people would rather see us serving than hear us preaching or whatever you call what we do in our services! I bet when we start serving, people will be more excited to listen to us preaching! Just saying. It's worth a shot.

I love how Jesus serves the crowd and the committed. He didn't run away when the people came near him. He encountered them. Remember the woman at the well? How about the lepers? What about the man who couldn't or didn't want to get into the pool? What about the five thousand and the four thousand? Jesus didn't call a caterer. He fed them. He taught his disciples how to serve. He broke the food, blessed the food, and handed it out. Knowing Jesus, he fished, too. He cleaned the nets as well. He served the Lord! Let me ask you: "Are you being a servant?"I'm not talking about taking out the trash at home. If you helped create the trash, take it out. If you're hungry-cook. If your clothes are dirty…wash them. I am talking about brushing shoulders with the sheep in your folds. I am talking about showing up to the Saturday Serve and laboring with the people in your church. I am not referring to you making an announcement and then never participating. Wait, I get it. Your church is way too big for you to serve now. You are paying staff for that, right? You have other people in charge of serving, right? You are afraid that by showing up to serve, you will get cornered for counseling or cornered for prayer or covered for really doing ministry. Yeah, it's tough serving people because they are needy. But God has placed you there to help meet a need. Serve! Develop boundaries, set guidelines, and tell those people you are here to serve alongside them and if they need extra time with you to make an appointment. I always tell people: "I love you, and I am here for you, but right now we are serving king Jesus and have to get some things done." I grab a shovel, a rake, a toilet brush, a mop, or whatever and get-to moving. I cannot stand on the platform Sunday to thank people for serving and pretend I know what they were doing.

I love to say we served together, we cleaned together, we prayed together, and we picked up trash together. I just believe that the shepherd leads by example, that's all. What about you? I know you have been the senior pastor for a hundred years there, but are you still a servant? Remember, they pay you to preach, counsel, pray, and visit! So you still have to find time to serve. Serving is separate from what you do to get a paycheck. Can I encourage you to go and find some feet to wash if this is you? If you are only doing and delegating and not serving, wash some feet. Start by washing your family's feet, the deacon's feet, maybe the Men's Ministry feet. I don't care whose feet you wash; just start washing. If you are not a pastor but an organizational leader, my advice is the same, be like Jesus and wash some feet; I promise you, you will never be the same.

Bill Johnson said, "Royalty is my identity. Servanthood is my assignment. Intimacy with God is my life source." Mahatma Gandhi said, "The best way to find yourself is to lose yourself in the service of others." I love this one by Harry S Truman: "It is amazing what you can accomplish if you do not care who gets the credit." The truth of the matter is that; "Leadership is about being a servant first." Allen West.

I hope you hear me loud and clear. It blows my mind how pastors have become protected from the people God has called us to serve. Tell your armor bearers to back down, don't serve from a distance, and stop being so untouchable. Go to the lobby and get to know your sheep. If you have ever wondered why they aren't following you, it's because they don't know the shepherd's voice, nor do they know his heart. It may be time to stop lecturing and start leading by example. Ok, I pray you get my point. You were called to serve, not to be served. If this humbles you, then make it your friend. Find some feet to wash today, weep before the Lord, repent, and start serving again. Love you. Mean it.

Questions for Discussion:

1- Whatever season of life you're in, you are a leader. Whether a parent, pastor, teacher, single person, or married. Believe it or not, people are watching you and looking at you as an example; we are all being watched. Ask yourself this honest question: What do people see when they see me?

2- Now that you have been honest, I hope you see yourself as a ten! Not what potential you have, but who you already are. What is one thing that, if you could change about yourself, you would change now?

3- Starting today, what are three things you can do to change that one thing?

Chapter 2

"Insta-famous"

Several years ago, there was a young man on our staff that was a student pastor. The craze of becoming popular on social media, especially Instagram, was beginning to take off. TikTok wasn't here yet, so pastors were using Instagram. Now, before you judge me and say I am just an old fuddy-dud, I use it too, but it doesn't drive my ego. I don't allow it to promote me. Going back to this past staff member, he was so driven to become like the other famous Instagram preachers that he neglected the current students at our church. How did I know this, you might ask? A trusted student approached me and said that this guy was more focused on getting followers on Instagram than encouraging and disciplining the students in our youth group. That was a shocker, coming from a middle schooler. So, I had to have a conversation with the pastor. Needless to say, that conversation fell on deaf ears and a hardened heart. This pursuit of Instagram popularity would eventually lead him down a path of moral failure by developing an Instagram relationship with a woman that wasn't his wife. In addition, that popularity pursuit led him down a very dark path which paid out with an affair. He was let go from our staff, but with tons of grace, counseling, encouragement, and even some severance. When we take our eyes off the real reason God has called us, we can end up going down a path we never dreamed we would go. It will keep us longer than we want to stay and charge us way more than we want to pay. In this case, not only did it affect him personally, but the effect had many ripples. Sometimes it seems as if pastors are attempting to store up more treasures on earth than storing up treasures in heaven. Now, I believe God has allowed us to do even greater things by utilizing social media as a platform for the Gospel. If Billy Graham used old-school technology to preach the Gospel, we should also use all we can get. But our use of technology has to be for the right reasons! We don't need it to boast about our underground parking spots, flaunt our first class airline tickets, or brag about our personal security details or our lavished lifestyles that can only be found on Life Styles of the Rich and Famous. Whom do we want to get the attention? Us or Jesus? Us or the Gospel? My platform or God's platform? Is it about my followers or those who are earnestly following Jesus? I am not hating on you or jealous of you, or even comparing myself to you. And, I certainly do not wish my followers would increase. There are most days that I consider myself a John the Baptist. I desire to point people to Jesus, not to Jason. I want people to know Christ, not me. I want their lives radically changed by the only one who can do that. Jesus.

Instagram has helped in many ways, but in many ways, it has brought significant downfall, disappointment, and despair to pastors, their marriages, and the church. If we spent more time ministering to people instead of hiding behind filters, we could potentially see revival. If we spent more time pastoring instead of posting, more lost people might meet Jesus. Hear me today. A servant is to promote his master, not the other way around. Who and what are you promoting on your social media? Are you caught up in this crazy world of more followers making you more popular? Has your focus on becoming an Instagram star distorted your focus on making Jesus famous?

"It's the world we live in." Yep, I hear this all the time, and it's why we justify it. When in Rome, do as the Romans. Add your analogy to the list. The issue I have is that pastors are so consumed with their popularity and notoriety that Jesus gets none of the spotlights. We tweet these catchy quotes in hopes that more people will re-tweet, re-share, and re-state them to increase the likes and followers on our page than them getting the intended message. I have been guilty of waking up on a Monday morning, grabbing my phone, and seeing who has shared my post, liked my post, and how many fire emojis I received. I know you have to, so don't judge me. I have realized that at the end of my ministry, it won't matter who liked it, but who God changed because of it. Am I more concerned with how the Holy Spirit uses the gifting inside of me to minister to those around me or those around me stroking the ego inside me?

Please hear me now. If you are reading this book, it is you who will have to share the message in this book with the Instagram preachers who will never read this book. The example we are leaving to the next generations of pastors is creating a fake culture for the Gospel message. The young pastors, the new pastors, and the blossoming pastors will attempt to make a name for themselves instead of the name that is above every name Jesus. Let us consider what the future will look like when we are dead and gone. What legacy are we leaving? A legacy of self followers or a legacy of Jesus followers.

Several years ago, my teenage son came to me and said, "Dad, you need to up your game on Instagram." I asked him, "Why?" He said, "If you ever want to preach at a huge conference, travel to other churches, and increase your followers, you better start posting more." I had a teachable moment with him right then and there. You see, he had started seeing these Instagram preachers rising to the surface, but he failed to see their potential downfall. I am by no means saying that if you are on Instagram, you will fall. You have the propensity to fall away from Jesus when it's all about you. Either way, I still have to ask my wife how to upload a picture to my story. I must be getting old! When I stand before Jesus one day, I want to hear the words, "Well done my good and faithful servant." I could care less to hear, "that was a sick post, and boy, you had lots of followers." I want to make Jesus famous! Once upon a time, kids wanted to be like pro athletes, firefighters, and police officers. Now, they want to be like the next hype worship leader, the next Instagram preacher, the next popular pastor. If I have heard it once, I have heard it a thousand times; "If I only had more followers, then I could be somebody." What a fake and phony world we live in today. Can you and I keep pointing people to the Savior and not to ourselves? I promise your likes from Jesus will increase. Remember, you're a tone setter. So set the right tone.

Questions for Discussion:

1- What example would others say that you are setting?

2- Losing focus on the main thing is one of the greatest tragedies someone can find themselves. If you have lost focus on what's important, how did you regain your focus? Write down the steps or processes you took to regain your focus.

3- Someone said, be a leader that's worth following. How can you be that leader that others want to follow?

Chapter 3

Your very first ministry, "Protecting Your Vineyard."

Song of Solomon chapter two, verse fifteen says: "Then you must protect me from the foxes, foxes on the prowl, foxes who would like nothing better than to get into our flowering garden." MSG. This verse is from the 'woman' in the relationship. It isn't ironic that 'she' says to protect her. 'She' can represent the marriage bed. 'She' can represent the bride of Christ. 'She' is to be protected at all costs. AT ALL COST! Put up a gate. Fortify the gate with barbed wire. Set up a protective barrier that surrounds her. This also means that you protect yourself from the foxes. Do you know what foxes do? They destroy the root system of your vineyard's blooming and blossoming vine. Have you ever heard the phrase Sly as a fox? They are incredibly sly. They are sneaky, unpredictable, cunning, and deceitful. They may look cute and cuddly until they bite and scratch you to pieces. They have beautiful coats but don't allow the outward appearance to fool you.

I heard another pastor's story asking Billy Graham to pray over his ministry. As Mr. Graham began to pray, he never mentioned his church, the choir, the staff, the growth of the church, or anything to do with the church. The pastor started wondering if Mr. Graham would get to that part in his prayer. But he never did. Mr. Graham spent most of his prayer asking God to protect his first ministry-his marriage and family. Savage! After the prayer, Mr. Graham told the pastor that his most important ministry was his wife and kids. Can I tell you that when you aren't your current Church's pastor, hopefully, your family will still be with you? I am by no means saying to disregard or give your church your leftovers, but I am saying that you give Jesus your most so you can love your wife and family the best. Let me ask you, do you prioritize your marriage? Why don't you stop reading and ask your spouse if you prioritize him or her? Hopefully, you're still breathing!

Now that you hopefully know the truth about your priorities, are you protecting your vineyard? That vineyard, in Jesus' name, is in full bloom. That vineyard is producing fruit. That vineyard is overflowing with health, blessing, and prosperity in Jesus. That vineyard should be a true reflection of the church. I believe one of the reasons non-churched people still aren't coming to church isn't because of the music selection. It isn't because the pastor has holes in his jeans. It isn't because the worship leader is tatted up. It isn't even because they ran out of cold foam in the church cafe. I believe it is because Christian marriages have ruined the portrait of what God intended the church to look like and for marriages to reflect. The reason why that may be the case is that we aren't protecting our vineyard. We would rather counsel every other broken marriage couple in the church rather than give our marriage attention. We say things like, what will the church think if I am not counseling every night of the week? What will the church think when your marriage is in disarray, and you have to have significant marriage counseling?

Leaders, do your church, your Jesus, yourself, and your marriage a huge favor and protect your vineyard. If it isn't being protected by you, who is protecting it? I can answer that for you; no one is! No one cares about your marriage and family as you should.

I like going to the gym because it helps me accomplish certain things. The gym motivates me; it helps release endorphins, it keeps my heart healthy, it keeps my skinny jeans fitting, but most importantly, it gives me strength and confidence to protect my wife and kids. I turn into the Hulk if you mess with them. We should have the same mindset when it comes to the bride of Christ. We should protect her from the foxes that ease into the vineyard, say they look adorable, and allow them to wreak havoc on the vines.

Seventeen years into my marriage, I realized that I was allowing the people of the church to zap the energy I used to have for my wife and kids. I didn't have any left in the tank for my family because I was pouring it out like a bucket with a million holes, and it would pour out twice as fast as I would be refueled. One Saturday, my wife and I were consumed with counseling a couple of families in our church when the dam broke. That Saturday morning, I looked at my wife and told her I was sick of the foxes we had allowed into our marriage. I told her I was going hunting. Sorry if you think foxes are too cute to kill.

Well, these foxes didn't have fur; they had death and defeat in their eyes and on their agenda. They wanted to distract my marriage, and they were doing a great job at it. They tried to divert our attention off of Jesus and each other to see that everybody else was our main priority. The Holy Spirit said to get at the gate entrance of your vineyard and start killing the foxes. Get them out of your marriage and family. They have overstayed their welcome, and it's time they go. So, I shut off the phone, the computer, and the TV and started saying no to many things, and God began healing my marriage and family. Thank you, Jesus! Since then, I have had to keep an eye out for the foxes because they keep coming. They multiply like rabbits.

Keep a close eye on your vineyard. Check the fruit often. Communicate to your spouse and kids because they will be honest. The people in your church will understand, and if they don't, oh, well. Seriously, they aren't caring for your vineyard as you will. Your vineyard is your first ministry, and God will hold us accountable for that. To the uprise of affairs, mistresses, secret rendezvous, flirtatious behavior, and the list goes on, say, "It must stop!" If you are in the habit of counseling the opposite sex, you are allowing foxes into your vineyard. Either have another woman present or don't counsel women. It's that simple. Going back to Billy Graham, he wouldn't even ride in an elevator with another woman unless another male was present or his wife was with him. Talk about protecting your vineyard. If you go out to lunch with an opposite-sex staff member that isn't your wife or daughter, you are allowing a fox in. You are giving the enemy an opportunity. I love my staff and look at the women as sisters, but I'm not having lunch with them. To me, that's inviting a fox into my marriage and ministry. I will fast before letting a fox in that way. If you travel alone, place many barriers around you so you don't fall into temptation. You are a leader, and the foxes want to destroy the leader. How much more trust would your spouse have in you if they went with you when you traveled out of town? How much more would your marriage grow and strengthen if you spent more quality time together? My wife is on staff, and we share an office. She sits right beside me. I see her all day, every day. That is not quality time for us. That is work mode, ministry mode, and get things done mode. We have to carve out time to spend together away from the office. When we do this, it's building stronger walls and more fortified gates to our vineyard. That is my first ministry, and I am called to protect, nurture, and groom it. God has entrusted me with my wife and kids to steward them to honor and glorify him. I'm catching the foxes because my vineyard is in full bloom! Remember these things as a tone setter. Go and set the right tone!

Questions for Discussion:

1- Is your vineyard worth protecting? I will answer that yes it is. Think about those in your vineyard. What extreme are you willing to take to protect them?

2- Take some time to slow down and see the foxes. Remember, they are sly and sneaky. What foxes can you identify? Be honest. What might not seem like a fox may very well be a fox.

Chapter 4

"Modern Day Aaron and Hur," Your Support System
is Everything.

"You will not quit until God releases you!"
This is what my friend and mentor told me. I had only
been in full-time ministry for about sixteen months
when I heard those words. At first, I was like, bro, you
have no clue what I have been going through for the
last seventeen months. To him, it didn't matter what I
was going through; he just knew that it wasn't going to
be wasted. Do you have those people you know who
will tell you the truth, no matter what? Think about it.
Who is it that God has surrounded you with that will
say the hard things to you, hold you accountable and
encourage you along the way? If you don't have that
someone, pray for that person today.

Had it not been for my friend, my wife, and a
pastor who had been through something similar, I
would have been long gone. These people help hold
your arms up. Do you remember the story in Exodus
chapter seventeen? It goes like this, "When Moses'
arms grew tired, Aaron and Hur brought a stone for
him to sit on, while they stood beside him and held up

his arms, holding them steady until the sun went down. In this way, Joshua defeated the Amalekites." You have to have those people who hold you "steady."

Many times in life and especially in ministry, we can get a little wobbly. We can be unsteady at times with all the negativity, the uncertainty, and having to keep up the façade. When Moses grew tired, weary, worn out, felt defeated, and felt like giving up, two close friends were there to help him. I have a couple of mentors or Aaron and Hurs, in several states and in my church. Sometimes I grow weary and think it would be better if I gave in.

At the moment, I think that I have to remember my calling. I must rely on these people to be by my side and hold up my arms. This is going to be essential to your health and your growth. You are only as strong as those that are doing life with you. If they are weak, you don't stand a chance. They have to be as strong or stronger than you are. They have to have the same calling, the same purpose, the same motivation, the same willingness, and the same heart to keep on keeping on. Listen, you aren't lesser because you need support. You are stronger than you think by admitting you need support. If you are a pastor or any kind of leader, it can get lonely. When we get lonely, we can isolate ourselves from others. I have never seen a shepherd isolate from his sheep. The shepherd is always with the herd. When the shepherd believes they don't need anyone because "they've got this," the enemy starts to devour them. The enemy won't provide a rock for you to sit on. He will take the rock and beat you while you're down.

Now, this is going to take some vulnerability on your part. You can't keep hiding behind the "Macho Man Randy Savage" mask and keep pretending everything is great. This is one of the main reasons there is a massive turnover rate of pastors today, and suicide is rampant. Pastors keep acting and putting up fronts to what's going on inside. When pastors take down the veil and allow people to see the real them, the real struggles, the real issues, I believe revival will break out. But I know what you are thinking; I am supposed to be the strong one to the weak ones. I am supposed to have it all together because I'm the one doing the counseling. I am the one they lean on in difficult seasons. If I don't have my mess together, we will have a church full of chaos. Well, praise Jesus! Jesus came for the sick, not the well anyhow. Now, I am not saying that you can continue to stay in your mess, throw pity parties, and preach all about your woes. The people want to know that you are human and that you rely on the Holy Spirit to help you make it through the day. So, what's it going to be? Are you going to keep flying solo, or are you going to call on your Aaron and your Hur? Trust me, they are waiting to help you stand.

As great as the opposite sex can be to tap into our emotions, don't fall into the trap. Let me say this again for the ones in the back. Don't fall into the trap. The most innocent of intentions can turn into the most devastating decisions. Your emotions tell you things to do that a sound mind would never. Do not trust your heart in these times of vulnerability. Don't have a best friend of the opposite sex unless it's your spouse. Trust me; you're opening up the gate of your vineyard and permitting a sly fox when this happens. I'm not calling that person a fox, but the enemy is more cunning than the foxes. He knows the emotional buttons to push; he knows what you think you are lacking, and he knows where to hit you the hardest. I have heard of many pastors and leaders falling into the trap of having the opposite sex as their Aaron and Hur. Don't do it. Your first ministry will suffer, and it's just an open the door to the enemy's schemes. Can I say, even if it's your sister-in-law or brother-in-law? You're better off not going down that road. You will thank me, I promise. You're a tone-setter, so set the tone.

Questions for Discussion:

1- Who is the person or people who are holding up your arms? Write their names down.

2- Why have you allowed them to have such a ministry in your life?

3- Do you currently have a person of the opposite sex as that person for you, other than your spouse? If you or they are married, consider remaining friends, but choosing another person to be that for you. I know it may be innocent, but the enemy operates most effectively in the innocent. How can you separate that relationship to keep it safe and create healthy boundaries?

4- Are you "wobbly" or a little unstable right now? Do you need your hands lifted and to be supported? Please be honest. You're not a superhero and it's ok. If you are a praying person, and even if you're not, please pray and ask God to show you that person who can be your Aaron. Write your prayer to God so you can look back and see whom He provided for you.

Chapter 5

Good v/s Bad Shepherds, "Shepherds don't beat their
sheep."

The Bible talks about Jesus being the Good
Shepherd. I think he is the greatest shepherd. He is
better than good; he is great. Jesus is the greatest
example to pastors because He was the most
outstanding pastor. Now, if Jesus is the good shepherd
and if he is the greatest example for other pastors/
shepherds/leaders to follow, why do some pastors and
leaders think it's right or even okay to beat the sheep? I
have been guilty of saying this and agreeing to this
statement: "If it weren't for people, the ministry
would be great." I repent for saying this. I am sorry
for ever thinking this. Forgive me for even letting this
phrase cross my lips. If it weren't for people, there
would be no need for shepherds or leaders. Shepherds
are only needed because there are sheep. Sheep need
direction. Sheep need accountability. Sheep need love
and grace. Sheep need a soft hand to hold them, not a
hard hand to beat them. A pastor's job is to love,
provide, and protect the sheep.

Remember Jesus asking Peter whether he loved him. Peter replied. " Yes, Lord," Jesus says to feed and love the sheep. Remember that? If not, read John chapter twenty-one. Did Jesus ever say beat my sheep, discourage my sheep, drag my sheep, hurt my sheep? No. If Jesus is our example, then we must follow his example. Have you ever sinned? Ok, that was a dumb question. And if you answered no to that question, repent now! So when you sinned, did Jesus beat you? Did Jesus drag you in front of the firing squad and shout 'fire?' When you fell short about thirty minutes ago, did Jesus shame you or make you feel guilty? If you felt any of those feelings, that was not from Jesus. That was from the devil. Jesus forgives, heals, pours out grace, lavishes us with acceptance, washes us in His blood, and gently restores us to fellowship with Him. Never once have I seen Jesus or read about Jesus beating a sheep. He went after the one that left the fold.

Good shepherds take care of their staff and those they are entrusted to lead. Good shepherds talk with their staff, not talk about their staff. Good shepherds speak life into their staff, not create death for them. Good shepherds gently restore them into fellowship, not shame them to repentance. Have you ever felt like the shepherd you are under treats you like a wolf instead of a sheep? They speak down to you and make you feel like a hireling instead of a co-laborer. They threaten you instead of defending you. They make you feel like you are just a task doer instead of a main player on the team. Have you ever asked those you lead if they ever felt this way from you?

Good shepherds always have their staff's backs. They always defend them. They never play favorites, nor do they highlight one over the other. Good shepherds never lay a hand on their sheep unless they are praying for them, helping them up, or encouraging them to get better. Listen, if you are a pastor or leader doing everything but these things, find a staff and strike yourself with it. Do it multiple times. This is what it feels like to be beaten by someone who is supposed to care, comfort, pastor, and love them. It doesn't make sense.

If you have had to hire several staff members for the same position and can't seem to get anyone to stick, the problem is most likely you. Wait, don't slam this book down. Go ahead; you paid for it! But for real, take a long look in the mirror at yourself first and then look at the condition of your sheep. If you have never asked to be involved in your staff's ministry, you might be a bad shepherd. If your staff walks around on eggshells around you, you might be a bad shepherd. If your staff shows up late, calls in sick, and makes every excuse in the book not to be at church, you might be a bad shepherd. If this is you, there is still hope for you. Look at the model of Jesus and just replicate what He did. Say what He said. Love the way He loved. Lead the way He led. Trust me, when you change, your staff will thank you. When you get better, those you lead will get better. You might not even think you are beating your staff or sheep. Ask your staff. Ask your leadership team how you are leading and have them be honest. You might not be hitting them with a real staff, but your words and nonverbal actions are. They leave as many bruises as a real staff does. Stop beating your sheep and start believing in them. You, my friend, are a tone setter. Go and set the tone.

Questions for Discussion:

1- Write out your description of a shepherd.

2- Now, write out the description of a shepherd that you want to be.

3- You are shepherding someone as a parent, leader, pastor, or mentor! Maybe it's a staff, a team, a company, or a business. How are you shepherding those "sheep?" Actually, how would they say you are shepherding people?

Chapter 6

Ministry is Messy, "Thick skin and a soft heart."

Have you ever felt like you were a door mat and have been trampled on repeatedly? I mean, by people who have great intentions but don't realize what they are doing to you? We often say at our church that activity ministry will always be messy. Ministry is messy because the more we reach people and welcome them into our world to point them to Jesus, the people (myself included) are always bringing mess with them! Ministry is messy, and ministry leaders can get caught up in that mess also. People often bring things with them into our worlds that affect us in a negative way, even when people do not mean any harm. One of the most outstanding books I have ever read is by Kevin Leman, and Bill Pentak called "The Way of The Shepherd." If you haven't read this book, finish mine first, and then go read that one! A dentist gave me this book, and it changed my life, my leadership, and how I treat people. It is so good that I have required my staff and elder team to read it. In this book, there is a statement that grabbed hold of my heart, and I can't seem to shake it. The book says, "Have thick skin and a soft heart."

So many times, we, as leaders, have thin skin and a hard heart towards the very resources God has entrusted us with. God's greatest resources are people. But often, instead of gently nudging people back into the pasture, we use a staff to aggressively move them into the field. Pastors and leaders are so guilty of this, especially when it comes to our team. We think that being a hardtail will go further and produce more work than actually constructive encouragement. When we have thin skin, everything will get on our nerves. In other words, everything people say will penetrate deeply. When this happens, we are short with our staff or team, our words hurt instead of heal, we place unmeetable expectations on them, and nothing they do is to our standard. It's a no-win situation. When you lead with thick skin and a soft heart, you will understand why your staff is the way they are. You can grow into the why and the how of the way they do things.

Here is an example. We have several millennials on staff….and I love it! And sometimes I hate it. I hate it when I am the one who gets worked up because they might not have done the work the way I would have. I get worked up when I feel like I am the only one working hard, and they are on their phones playing black ops. Our staff was going through a trying time about three years ago, and I had asked God to restore laughter and joy into the hallways of our office. One day I was pounding away at my work, and all of a sudden, the loudest, most contagious noise shook my office. I pushed back from my desk and thought, somebody is about to catch these hands! That is a joke, by the way. I should have said, I am about to stop all this noise so we can get some work done. As I made my way to my door, it was obvious the sound that had interrupted me was actually exuberant laughter! Right then, the Holy Spirit gently said, "you asked for this. Now sit the flip down and laugh! (Emphasis added.)" He didn't say sit down, but He did say I am answering your prayer! I am restoring the joy to this staff. I am doing a new work in these walls. Embrace the laughter and know that the work will be accomplished.

It freed me y'all. After realizing that God had answered my prayer, I walked out of my office, laughed with them, and thanked them for laughing. That may have been a mistake because from then on, it never stopped! To this day, we have a very joyful workplace, and we have even made laughter a core value on staff! Thick skin will allow you to see the gifting in your team, champion the call on their lives and help to manifest those gifts. By allowing the Holy

Spirit to soften my heart in understanding, it allowed my skin to be thick and for the circumstance to bounce right off of me. Don't let things penetrate you so deeply! Oftentimes, things are not that serious. When I understood this, my leadership became freer, and I found myself celebrating the differences this staff offers this house.

Ministry gets messy when you micromanage your staff. Oh boy, here we go. Are you a micromanager? When I started this church, which is only eight years old, I had an issue with micromanaging. And it was only two staff members; me and the worship leader. You realize real quick that this style of leadership will kill you, drain you, and make your staff miserable. I served under this type of leader years ago in Charlotte, NC. This pastor would make me do homework. He wanted me to turn in projects to him weekly for discipleship, outreach, family ministry, etc. I couldn't even do my job because I was so busy trying to complete academic projects for him. And to top it all off, when I would turn in the project, he would make sure it was on time and then do absolutely nothing with it. He didn't think being a student pastor and family pastor was enough work for me. It reached the point that I was either becoming his student or the pastor of students. He didn't like it when I suggested that because now he couldn't control me as much. He couldn't keep his thumb on me when I would visit middle and high schools. I had to do ministry instead of projects. So, if this is the type of leader you are or are becoming, my advice to you is: Stop! You may have some insecurities, and that's why you are micromanaging. Another thing, if you have to micromanage, then you might have to reevaluate your staff. Micromanaging will take you off from mission and vision. You will be so focused on what your team is or isn't doing that you can't do what God has called you to do. On the flip side, if you are being micromanaged, you may or may not be doing what you are supposed to. There could be a reason, other than your leader's control, that you need to be led this way. Either way, if you can get away from this type of leadership, the better and more productive you will be, and you will sleep a lot better, too.

Check your skin. Ask God to thicken it to the things that don't matter the most. You may be lessening your time in the ministry by having thin skin. Ask God to soften your heart to the differences he has aligned to support you on this mission. Different is good, so I encourage you to keep changing. Don't ever hire everyone like you. This is probably why

your spouse is still with you-they are is nothing like you! If you surround yourself with your personality, you are defeating the purpose of each body part having a role in completing the task God has for you. They are different for a reason. The more diverse your team is, the greater your chances of accomplishing more significant goals for the kingdom of God you will.
 This is a principle I am trying to continue to live by.
 So, have thick skin and a soft heart. Your team will once again thank you. You're a tone setter. Go and set the tone!

Questions for Discussion:

1- What's the current thickness of your skin? Is it fragile or is it tolerable for more stretching?

2- How is your heart? Not the physical wellness of it, but how is your heart toward those you lead and serve? How is your heart toward your spouse? How is it toward your kids? How is it toward co-workers, neighbors, and supervisors? Be honest and write down how your heart is toward them.

3- How can you change your heart so that it becomes soft? How can your heart become softer toward those you lead? Write down three things that you can start today.

Chapter 7

"A present and future word"

I pray that something you have read has made you realize that you haven't arrived. I wrote this book, but, trust me, I am nowhere near where I want to be as a leader. I have made tons of mistakes, but thankfully less than before. I hope you can receive one nugget of truth from my story so it doesn't become your story. I hope you can commit to rewriting your history and stop repeating it. You don't have to be like the leader you have been led by. One of a leader's greatest tragedies is discouraging the next layer of leadership. One of the greatest triumphs is to help raise the next layer of leadership. God wants us to empower others. He wants us to release others. He desires us to call out gifting and champion someone else's passions. A great leader will do this. A threatened leader will not. Let's cut to the quick for a second. Give the most honest answer you can to this question: Is there a current staff member or team member that intimidates you? Wait, Before you are so quick to answer, be truthful. If there is someone whom you are threatened by, why? If you are the senior pastor and the youth pastor is a threat to you, why do you feel this way?

Let me say this; I have had a youth pastor who preached better than me, he was more intelligent than me, and the people loved him. What he couldn't do was pastor well, manage finances, or be efficiently organized. But guess what, instead of being intimidated, I utilized him. I put him in a preaching series with me. I celebrated him and shouted him down when he would preach. I would make him feel like the hero.

TD Jakes said, "Sometimes you have to let someone else bring out the casserole." Even if you baked it, let someone carry it to the table. You might have even purchased the ingredients, slaved over the stove, but let someone else carry it out. The guests might give that person all the credit, but you know who put in the labor. That person is on your TEAM for a reason. And you probably hired them. Don't stick a team player in the corner; tell them what to do, how to do it, and why you are threatened. You are on the same team!

The worst thing a senior pastor or any leader can do is be intimidated by a team member. This is horrible leadership; the next thing that will happen is you will be hiring a new youth pastor or trying to fill a position. I promise you that they will not stay around long if . Utilize them. Celebrate them. If they threaten you, ask them to join you in a series. Ask them to help you. Ask them to give you some fresh ideas. It is fantastic when this happens. And when you finally allow them to preach in "big church," sit on the front row and don't go out of town. Sit on the front row, stand and clap, shout them down, and make much of them.

The only time I ever got to preach in a "big church" was when that pastor went out of town-one time! After my message, a sweet woman came up to me and said, "That was some amazing preaching, son." "The Holy Spirit moved me." My reply to her was, please don't tell the pastor. He will never give me that chance again. Well, you guessed it. The following week after he returned to the church, I was called into his office. Once again, instead of celebrating what God had accomplished, he reminded me that there was only one pastor at that church, and it wasn't me. I promise to God that was his exact words. That's why I will never be that way. That is how NOT to be a pastor and leader.

Let me share this jewel with you. After I graduated from seminary, while on staff at the church in Charlotte, my in-laws gave me a pen plaque for my desk that had my name on it: "Pastor Jason Smith." I was so hesitant to put it on display because I just knew what this joker would do. He had walked through my office without me being there because he walked in and asked me what was on my desk one day. I very timidly said, oh, just a gift my in-laws gave me for graduating. He touches it and begins to tongue-lash me for even having it on my desk. When he walked out, you can only imagine how I felt. I had just accomplished a major task, and my "pastor" didn't celebrate it. At that point, I couldn't get out of there quick enough.

The point I am trying to make is to take this as a warning. Take this as a wake-up call. Take this and measure yourself up to the Good Shepherd, Jesus. Did he treat his sheep this way? Did talent and good leaders threaten him? Jesus knew the condition of his sheep. Jesus cared, loved, and even carried his sheep! Jesus never beat his sheep or bruised his sheep. Jesus died for his sheep. He gave up his life for his sheep. Are you willing to die for the sheep he has placed in your pasture? Do you have the strength to even carry sheep that are more talented than you? Will you get the necessary help to get better, lead better, serve better, and live better? I pray that the Holy Spirit will use this book to show you how NEVER to be a pastor or leader. I would love to hear from you, to pray for you, and maybe to share deeper into my story with you. My email is

jason@latitude.church. I am truly here for you.

The church God has called me to pastor is Latitude Church in New Bern, NC. We are an eight-year-old church plant and have seen a move of God never like before. I am more excited to lead her than when God first called me to plant her. I have seen heartache, and my heart has been incredibly blessed. I am ready to lead. I am prepared to set the tone for what's next for my life, marriage, family, and ministry. You, my friend, are a tone-setter, too. Lift up your team and those around you, especially when they are better than you! Our present and future world depend on our ability to carry our sheep! Go and set the tone.

Questions for Discussion:

1- Write down the people's names that you currently lead. After each name, ask yourself, do I know their condition? Do I know how they are really doing?

2- What are three ways that you can start to know your sheep? Write three practical ways to get to know their passions, strengths, and gifting.

3- Is there someone that is a threat to you that you lead? Why do you feel this way? Pray and have a healthy conversation with them about it. They may feel the same way about you. Ask God to heal any animosity between you.

Chapter 8

"Repentance leads to revival."

You may not be a fan of the Bible, but that's okay. You may not even be a person of faith. You may have liked the cover of this book, or someone purchased it for you, and now you're obligated to read it. I hope that one day you will consider faith in Jesus. Either way, regardless of what you think or have heard about the Bible, or what faith in Jesus is all about, I want to share a verse with you. I may have mentioned it in a previous chapter as well. Romans 2:4 tells us, "or do you show contempt for the riches of his kindness, forbearance, and patience, not realizing that God's kindness is intended to lead you to repentance?" (NIV.). Lean in with what I am about to tell you because some of you may feel shame, condemnation, and guilt because of some of your behavior. God is not mad at you. He hasn't turned his back on you. God is in pursuit of you right now. He is a loving, kind, generous, and a grace-giving father. Let me say it again; God isn't mad at you. There is nothing that you can do or not do that will change the way He loves you.

This verse says that his loving kindness leads you, not pushes you, not forces you to repent. His love should compel you and me to turn from our sin, do an about-face, and start moving toward him. I love this about the character of God. It doesn't matter what you have done up to this point; His mercy and grace are available to you and are sufficient for you. Repent means going in a different direction than you are currently going. I like to say that repentance is a daily posture of our faith. I have to repent daily because I find myself going in the wrong direction. Once I repent, I am restored, and my faith is strengthened. Repentance isn't a one-time expression. Repentance is a daily reminder of the love that God has for us.

I am unsure how you pray, if you pray or what you are praying for, but I have been praying for revival to happen in my lifetime. I am not talking about the three, ten, or even one hundred people that get saved at an Easter service or Christmas. Those are miracles, and we celebrate them. I am talking about when God visits you and your church, business, or family, and something radically changes and perhaps receives new life. Revival means to give life back to what was once living. Revival isn't for people who have never given their hearts and lives to Jesus. Revival is for those people who have been saved but now are not living as if they were saved. They have either gone a different direction or back to where Jesus found them. Revival happens when God's people pray. Revival happens when God's people repent of their sins. Revival happens when God's people deny evil, shame the devil and start living in the newness of Jesus.

Let's get real for a moment. What if pastors and leaders repented from their sins? Think about it. Pastors and leaders are telling everybody else where to go, how far to go, and what to do to live a holy and pure life. But who tells them? Who are pastors and leaders listening to so that they are encouraged and corrected? Oh boy, here we go.

Correction isn't a trait that most likely any of us hold close. Correction corrects us. Boy, that was brilliant. Correction should inspire us. It should empower us. It should free us. Correction isn't always wrong, but when it's received with a spirit of humility, it will set you free. Do you think you need correction? The Bible again says that a loving father disciplines his children. I should be loved like nobody's business if that's the case. My daddy used to tear this behind up! I am thankful today that he did. It didn't hurt me at all. It helped to mold me into who I am today. My dad loved me enough to correct me. He cared enough for my future to correct my present. Correction leads to the narrow road. Can I tell you that correction is lonely, and not many people choose its path? But when you select correction, you are wise, live long, and are joyful. At least that's what the Bible says. And by the way, I believe it. I heard a long time ago that whatever keeps you humble, make that your friend. I want to add that whatever keeps you corrected, make that your best friend. Correction isn't comfortable at the time, but it becomes great after time. I want to challenge you to allow others to offer correction to you. I don't mean to nit-pick you apart. I mean those people you trust, love, and walk close with; allow them to offer you correction. You're not above it. Maybe you need some correction. One of the greatest moments of my entire ministry was when a teenager corrected me, and it happened to be my son. He said, dad, "You spend more time with other people you don't know than with your own sons." After I picked myself up from the floor, I repented. I told him that he was right and that God used him to correct me. Some of us would have justified our absence, but I couldn't. He was right. All I could do was offer forgiveness and reprioritize my time. I accepted his correction, and it helped to change my life and our relationship. When pastors and leaders receive correction with humility, there will be repentance. When repentance happens, there will be revival. I believe we will see our businesses thrive, our families prosper, our marriages healed, and our churches flourish. We may not even have to spend another dime on more lights, more stage props, or giveaway tee shirts. This may be the answer to the budget dilemma that you've been facing. You don't need more money, just more repentance. You don't need another staff member, just more repentance. You don't need a new building, just a new heart. You don't need more speakers or better singers, just more repentance. Ask God to search your heart right now. It doesn't matter if you're in Starbucks, Heavenly Grounds, or He-brews Coffee Shop. Shoot, if you're in Chick-fil-A, somebody might buy you a milkshake if they see you weeping at the table from repentance! What if the people in the church or business you lead need to see their leader broken before God? How do you think they will respond? Either way, God's response is acceptance, healing, and restoration. He doesn't judge you; he loves you. Take some time and repent. Take some time to read Proverbs 4. It says, "take time, stop, listen and embrace what the Lord has to say to you."

Be ready for God to pour out His blessings and power over your life, church, and business. You are a tone setter, so don't wait for your elders, deacons, trustees, VP, supervisors, or managers to repent. You be the catalyst. You be the first one to set the tone for them. I guarantee that the tone you set with repentance will be the tone that helps to better them. You're a tone setter. Go and set the tone.

Questions for Discussion:

1- If you're like me, there are things in your life that are not in line with God's will and desires for your life. If so, take a moment and write those down.

2- Look at that thing or that list that you wrote from question one. Repentance means to turn from that and go in a new direction. Whether you are a person of faith or not, choose to go in another direction. Walk away or run away from that thing that is holding you back.

3- After you have made your list and hopefully turned from those things, thank God for helping you. You may think you don't know how to pray, so let me teach you; just open up your mouth and talk to God like you're having a conversation with him. He isn't impressed with our prayer vocabulary, so just talk to Him. He is ready and willing to listen. Doesn't that feel good?

Chapter 9

"Practice the fruit of self-control"

Just because you are the boss, the president, the CEO, CPO, or the HPIC (head person in charge), doesn't mean that you have free reign to do as you wish. We all need accountability. Tone setters lead by example. They don't lead by saying, "do as I say, not as I do." Tone setters "do." They practice what they preach. They live by example. Now, if you don't want to set the tone for your company or those you lead, that's your choice. But, by the time you get to this chapter, maybe you have had a change of heart. Hopefully, you are experiencing freedom and healing. Hopefully, you are feeling great about yourself and have witnessed some changes in yourself. Why does the head person seem to think they can't be or don't want to be held accountable for their actions or the lack of them? Yes, Jesus is my boss. I am a pastor, but there are more levels to my accountability. I can't just tell people I answer to Jesus; nobody else matters. I have to show people that I have to live by example as a tone setter. I have surrounded myself with a staff that has been given permission to correct me, if needed, and to hold me accountable. My two sons have been given permission that if they see me talking with another woman that isn't their mother, to walk up into our conversation, introduce themselves, and ask who she is. That might sound rude and a little too much, but what's my integrity worth? What is my character worth? What is my reputation worth? I have to be above reproach. I have to protect my own vineyard. I have to pray for protection over my marriage and family. I must guard against evil and everything the world throws at me. I have a huge target on my back for the enemy of my faith to attack. I have to keep up walls. I can't call or text other women. I can't, nor want, another woman being my best friend. Of course, my wife and I have issues, but I will not confide in another woman. I am asking for a possible emotional affair. I am opening up a door to inappropriate behavior. I am inviting someone else into my vineyard that doesn't need an invitation to come in. Men, women, leaders, pastors, etc., practice self-control. No one can keep you under control but you. I know your spouse has tried. Mine has but to no avail. My wife doesn't know my mind. She can't control me or my thoughts. I have to surrender my mind and heart to Jesus daily to keep myself under control. Though I am a pastor, I am still human and all man. This means I have to put things in place to protect myself. You have to put things in place to protect yourself. That may mean not hiring that young, attractive, single secretary. She might be well qualified, but you know you. That might mean that your employee meetings have to take place with your door open to your office or have another person sit in with you. That might mean you don't meet or counsel the opposite sex after hours. That might mean that you draw the line and not cross it. That might mean your corporate parties do not get carried away with too many adult beverages. Have self-control. You are a tone setter, and your tone will be the tone that others will follow. If you don't practice self-control, you will create an environment where people are out of control. If you are currently living an out-of-control life and leading an out-of-control company, employees, or staff, listen closely; get yourself together. Begin right now practicing self-control. It is ok to say no to lunch with the opposite sex. I know what you may be thinking, it's already planned, and I can't back out now. Sure you can. Tell them you are practicing self-control, and there will no longer be luncheons or meetings like these. You may have to reset the tone. Be the leader worth following and reset it if need be. I am a member of a gym in town, and women workout in there. And if you are a gym member, you know what I mean right now. They like to work out in extremely tight clothing. I get it. I just have to protect my eyes from lusting when I see them. I can't use certain equipment if they are near it. I have to be intentional when working out, so I am not losing self-control. Even if it means I must change up my workout or get on the dreaded treadmill. I hate that thing! If you are struggling with self-control, go to the extreme. Seriously, you will be glad that you did. Most marriages fail because of the lack of self-control from one or both spouses. The majority of affairs start because of a lack of self-control. Most business owners, pastors, and leaders' reputations are ruined because of a lack of self-control. You are a tone setter. As you practice self-control, you will be placing yourself under control, and the more you are under control, the greater influence you will have on others' self-control. You're a tone setter. Go and set the tone.

Questions for Discussion:

1- What areas seem out of control to you right now?

2- Since you have some control over those situations, what steps can you put in place to help regain your self-control?

3- Be a leader that takes responsibility. How can you start to be more responsible in the area of self-control?

4- What barriers and healthy boundaries can you create today to protect you from making decisions that could harm your character and career?

Chapter 10

"The Prescription"

I cannot end this book without giving you the prescription. Anytime you have visited the doctor's office for being sick, you most likely leave there with a prescription for medication. That medication is designed to make you feel better, relieve an itch or provide relief from pain. The drug I want to write for you is what Dr. Jesus prescribed for me. Even if you're not a person of faith, please finish this book.

If you have ever been treated like an unworthy, useless, lowlife by a leader/pastor, etc., you probably know what it might be. After hearing my heart, seeing some of my passions, and experiencing some of my frustrations, you understand. You might think it includes an Easton aluminum baseball bat or a Rambo survival knife, but it's actually the opposite. Your prescription is forgiveness. Jesus prescribed forgiveness for me. The new "F" word! I had to choose, every day, to forgive. Not only did I have to choose to forgive, but I also had to walk in that forgiveness. I had to relive that forgiveness daily. I am aware that so many of the things we are today are because of who we had around us yesterday. We are often as healthy as those who influenced us, and if you are like me, you often needed better examples of a true tone setter. Some days, my mind will wander to yesteryear, and I have to choose to forgive people all over. The moment I think, how could I have been treated this way, I have to forgive. When I choose to forgive, and when you decide to forgive, it's liberating. The Bible even says that we can't be forgiven if we don't forgive. And, I want to be forgiven! Don't you? I have to take three forgiveness pills daily for the rest of my life and sometimes at a very high dose. Now, I know what some of you are thinking. I know how you are being treated. I understand that you are hurt, have scars, and have lost years off of your ministry. I can empathize with your hurt, frustration, and sleepless nights. I can absolutely wrap my mind around the disappointments and pain associated with how you have been treated. Even still, forgiveness is for you, not them. Forgiveness frees you from bondage. Forgiveness provides a sense of relief and healing that you might not experience without it.

Forgiveness doesn't mean that you have to have dinner with that person or that you have to be hospitable and have them in your home. Forgiveness doesn't mean that you have to trust them again. Forgiveness is the prescription to your joy and freedom in Jesus. Here is what I know about the Bible; it never says I have to forgive and forget. And if you find that, I will repent and write a new book on how Biblically illiterate I am! I always tell people that God will never ask you to get over something, but He will always help you get through something. There is a significant difference between getting over and getting through. Getting through is depending on the Holy Spirit to provide you with the ability to forgive, the ability to move on, and the ability to continue forgiving. When your flesh wants to fight, the Spirit says to forgive. When your mind tells you to hang on to all of those negative thoughts, the Holy Spirit tells you to take captive those thoughts and to renew your mind. I will never be able to forget the way I have not been pastored and shepherded, but I have chosen to forgive those who didn't fulfill their role. I have refilled my prescription many times, and I am sure it will never expire.

Listen, I know it's painful, unfair, and not how it's supposed to be. If anyone can relate, this guy can. In the name of religion, I will never discount the ungodly ways that you have been mistreated, but I know forgiveness will help. You may even need to forgive a parent, pastor, or mentor. I will never say, "suck it up; life isn't fair." I will always show grace to those struggling under a narcissistic, egomaniac's leadership. I know your flesh can only take so much, and then you choose to either run, fight or get in the fetal position and cry. I have learned an important principle in my years of ministry and life. You need to write this down, take it to Hobby Lobby and have it matted, and mount it on your wall for the entire world to see: TRUTH NEEDS NO DEFENSE, AND A LION NEEDS NO DEFENDER! You are welcome, my friend! Seriously, you will sometimes think you are losing your marbles and that you are the crazy one (maybe you are), but always know that you don't have to defend the truth. The truth will always defend itself, and that is freeing. Take a moment today and every day for the rest of your life and choose to forgive. Say the names of those people out loud to God. Forgive each one; don't pray they get the flu and die. How did that feel? Still, hurts? Yep, it will. I promise that one day you will think back over those times and say these words: "it had to happen that way." I am better for it. I am greater for it. God has propelled me forward because of it. I can now relate to others and provide counsel, love, and support. God, I choose to forgive because you chose to forgive me. On occasion, you might have to visit your neighborhood pharmacy, walk to the clerk and ask for a refill. When they ask for what, just smile and tell them, "I need to refill my forgiveness." God bless you, my friend, and keep your eyes fixed on Jesus. Until next time, remember, You are a tone setter. Go and set the tone! We are Tone Setters.

Questions for Discussion:

1- OK, let's revisit some people who have hurt you. Wait! I want this exercise to help you forgive them. Forgiveness is your choice to be free and to have peace. Write their names down, and next to their names, write this: "I forgive you." If it makes you feel better, write; "F" you. That means forgive you!

2- After you have written this down, I want you to say those people's names out loud and then say I forgive you. (You may want to be alone when you do this, so the person next to you doesn't hear this).

3- Write down how this made you feel. Be honest

4- Now, put this on repeat. This isn't a one-time and done exercise. You may have to do it daily for many weeks. Just like taking your real medication, remember to do this daily. I promise the more you do this, the more freedom you will feel.

P.S. If this book has helped you, please give a copy to someone else. I know I am not a famous author, but maybe coming from a redneck preacher, they will understand something differently. Go set the tone!!

ABOUT THE AUTHOR

Jason Smith is currently the senior/lead pastor of Latitude Church in New Bern, NC. He has been a pastor for over fifteen years. He just started his leadership journey on John Maxwell's leadership team. He has been a guest speaker at several churches and plans to increase his influence outside of the four walls of the church. He holds an undergraduate degree and a master's degree from Liberty University in Religion and Sociology. He has written two other books; Possessing the Promise and Ever Be On My Lips. For more information about him visit tonesetters.me or email him at jason@latitude.church.

NOTES

Made in the USA
Columbia, SC
16 September 2022

66796948R00043